THE DARK BROWN GIRL
Book of Affirmations

WRITTEN AND ILLUSTRATED BY

ASHA V. NTIM

Founder of the Chrysalis Program

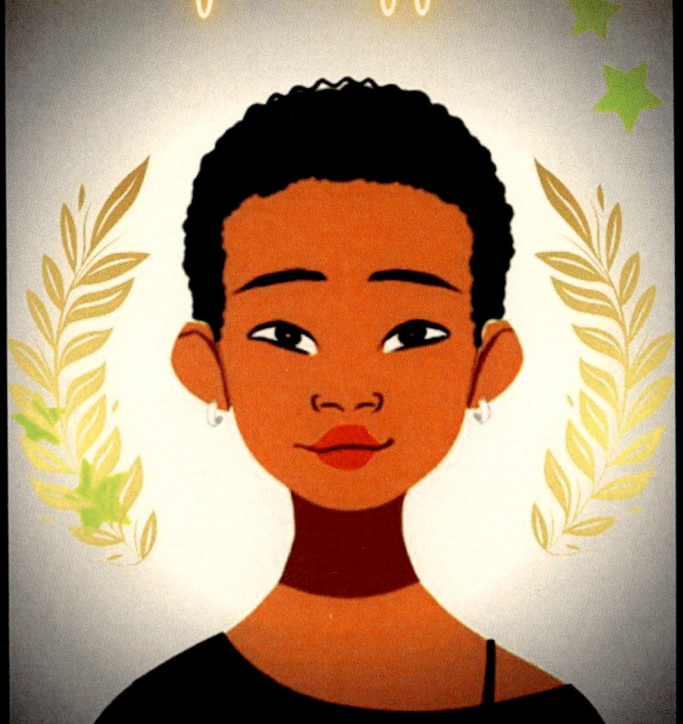

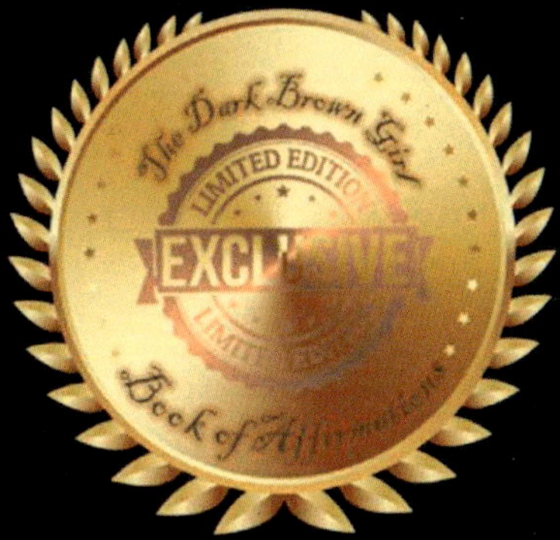

To Every Girl

Because your words have

POWER

Daily Affirmations

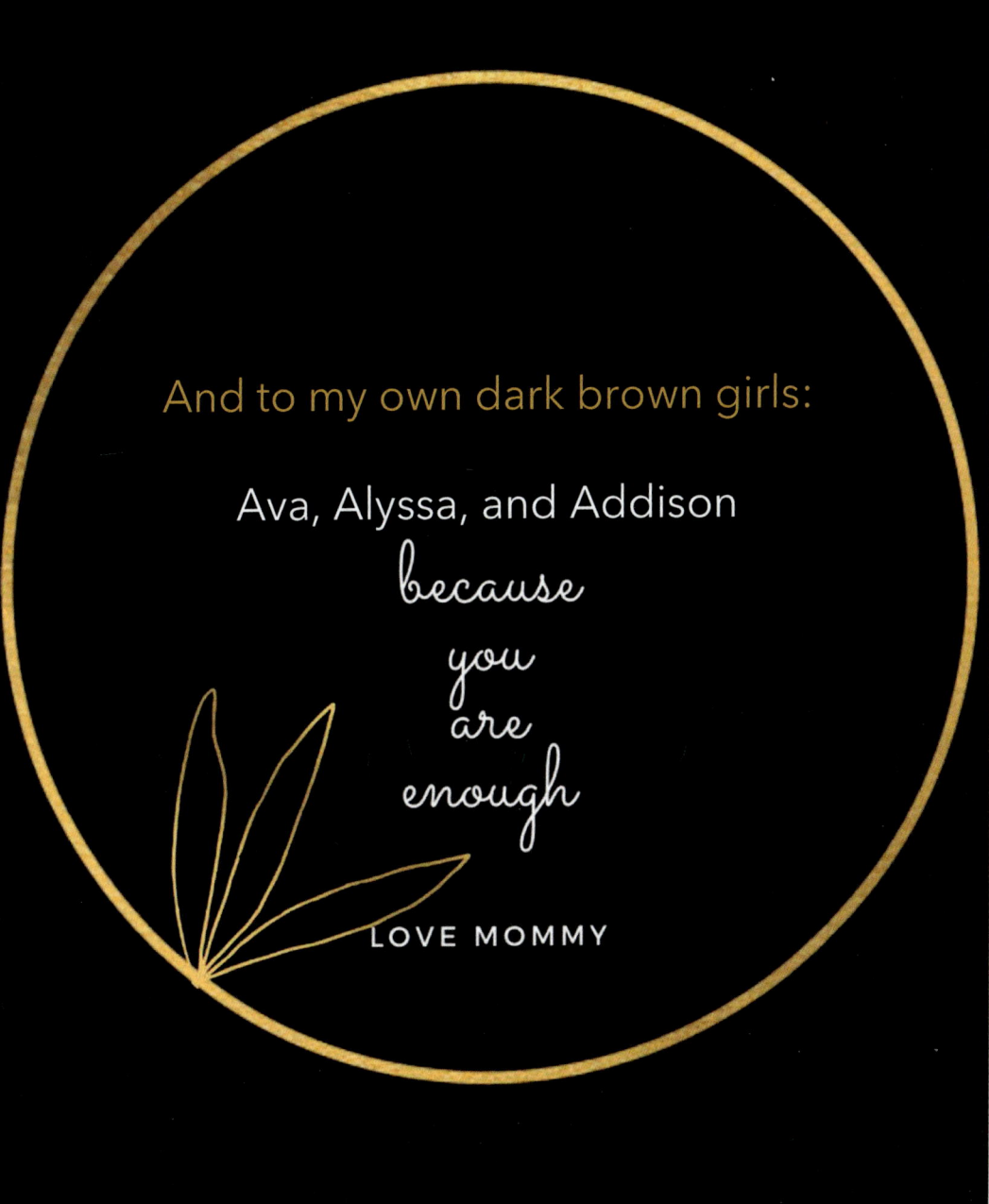

And to my own dark brown girls:

Ava, Alyssa, and Addison

because you are enough

LOVE MOMMY

I am beautiful.

I am strong.

I am fearless.

I belong.

I stand out.

I am honest.

I am proud.

I am a goddess.

I am magical!

I am brilliant.

I am powerful!

I am resilient.

I love my skin.

I love my hair.

I am a loyal friend.

I am rare.

I am capable.

I am accepted.

I am unbreakable.

I am protected.

I am forgiven.

I have wisdom.

I can tell what's real

from what isn't.

I am tough.

I am free.

I am wealthy.

I will succeed.

I am confident.

I know who I am.

I have talents and gifts.

I believe that
"I can."

I was created

in the image of God.

My words bring life

because I have what I say.

I vow to affirm

myself everyday.

Affirmation Deep Dive

Beautiful

What does it mean to be beautiful?
Where do we learn how to define what is beautiful against what isn't?

Beauty begins within. There is beauty in the way you think, learn, live and love.
You are beautiful.

Strong

What does it mean to be strong?
What are some ways we display strength in our every day lives?

Fearless

Why is it important to be fearless?
Having courage will allow us to stand up for what you believe in. Being brave enough to use our voice is so important.

Belonging

Knowing that we belong is an important part of building self confidence. Historically African American girls and women have been made to feel there are spaces we do not belong.
Whatever the space, we belong. We are worthy.

Stand Out

What does it mean to stand out?
We aren't shrinking ourselves to blend into the crowd. It's ok to be our full selves. We don't have to be like anyone or everyone else. We are proud to be authentic and that makes us stand out.

Honest

Being honest is important because it allows for closer quality friendships and relationships. It builds trust and confidence. Honesty has been linked to improved physical health and less stress, anxiety and depression.

Proud

What does it mean to be proud?
Celebrate yourself. All that you are. Celebrate even your seemingly small accomplishments.

A Goddess

What makes one a goddess?
A female Deity. Divine.
A woman who is adored.

Magical

Black people are magical. This isn't up for debate or discussion. We are able to transform. We reinvent ourselves every generation into being the most imitated people on earth. Whatever we touch succeeds. We are magical.
"Just because we are magical, doesn't mean we aren't real." Jessie Williams

Brilliant

We are brilliantly creative, innovative, clever, and talented.
We are also brilliant because of how our light shines radiantly.

Powerful

We are powerful: unstoppable. Intense.
Unmovable in our convictions. Focused. Influential.

Resilient

We are tenacious. Our bounce back game is strong.
No matter what this life throws us, we rise above it.
We don't just rise above we thrive.

Skin and Hair

We have been taught by American Standards of beauty that our skin and hair make us less attractive.
We aren't beautiful in spite of our blackness and our coarse hair; we are beautiful because of it.

Rare

Because there is no one like you. You are an original. Everything about you is uniquely and strategically designed. You are perfectly you.

Capable

There is nothing you cannot accomplish.

Accepted

We don't need to worry if we will be accepted by others. We are enough. We are equipped with everything we need to be successful, happy and fulfilled.

Protected

It is important that our black women and children are protected. We speak this into existence. That we will remain safe and away from hurt, harm or danger.

Forgiven

Affirming that we are forgiven is important as we allow our past mistakes to dictate the way we see ourselves. We start to believe that the world sees our vulnerabilities and that affects our self image. Saying we are forgiven reminds us that we are not our mistakes. We are forgiven by God, by others, and by ourselves.

Wisdom

Wisdom is the application of knowledge. Having wisdom will help us to make better decisions. Wisdom allows us to use our intuition to lead us in the right direction; to not just know what is right, but to also do what is right.

Discernment

Discernment is such an important gift that we already possess. It allows us to see people and situations as they really are instead of how we wish them to be. Discernment will save us from heartbreak, manipulation, and harm. Let us be able to use our discernment to tell what is real from what isn't

Enough. I Love Myself

I am enough of whatever I need in any given moment. I love everything about me. I celebrate the things I do well. I see an opportunity to improve instead of seeing flaws.

Tough

The "tough" we are affirming is not the kind of tough that starts fights.
This tough is a indestructible tough.
A bold confident tough.

Free

We are free. Free to choose who we want to be. To do not necessarily to do what is expected, but we are free to pave a fresh new path; create a new mold because sometimes there isn't a blueprint. We may need to create one.

Wealthy

Wealthy refers not only to financial affluence, but every area of our lives. We can be wealthy in love, peace, and family or friends.

Succeed

Success can be defined by each of us individually. Some define success by traditional standards. We can choose what success looks like to us. When you achieve happiness, peace, contentment. That place for me, is success.

Healthy

Healthy usually refers to physical health. For me, health describes mental health, emotional health, spiritual health. How healthy is our decision making? How healthy are our relationships? How well do we treat ourselves and others?

Confident

Even if you don't feel confident, saying that you feel confident enough will eventually convince your mind that you. Continue to say it until you believe it.

Know who you are

Knowing who you are will allow you to make unbiased decisions unable to be negatively influenced

Talents and Gifts

Each one of us is uniquely talented. We have gifts that are in the inside of us that just need to be nurtured, practiced, and cultivated. What you feed will grow. Choose what you spend your thoughts and time.

"I Can"

"Whether you believe you can or you can't, you're right."
"I can" is a powerful statement because what ever you place behind it defines your capability. If only you believe and are willing to put in the work… You Can.

Smart

Smart can be defined in many ways. Academic ability is important. Equally important is making smart decisions and being emotionally intelligent.

Work Hard

We affirm that we will work hard because there are some things in the life that we cannot have any other way.
This affirmation reminds us to be determined and driven. Working hard could mean, doing what we don't feel like doing in the moment to get a result that we desire long term.

In God's Image

We are created in God's image to not only to reflect his deity, but His heart. As God is perfect, we affirm to love perfectly; to forgive and create. To build relationships and not destroy. To change the world around us for the better. May each being who encounters us be better than it was before.

I am...

"I am" are the two most powerful words because whatever comes behind them shape your identity. We have the ability to name ourselves; not just what we believe that we are, but who we want and choose to be.

Speak life over yourself daily. There will be temptation to believe the bad. Choose the good for yourself. Choose the good for one another. Choose the good for our future.

Author's Thoughts

The Book of Affirmations was the first children's book I authored, written to empower dark brown girls. This 5 Year Anniversary Edition commemorates the achievements The Dark Brown Girl movement has made since it was written. We have sparked a conversation that has changed the world one readers at time.

ABOUT THE BOOK OF AFFIRAMTIONS

The Book of Affirmations is intentionally written for my oldest daughter after hearing colorist remarks made toward her. My self and my husband having experienced colorism as children, decided to be vigilant in my molding of her self esteem. After releasing this book of affirmations, many parents began to reach out for support for their daughters who struggled with self image. The need for support and community developed my nonprofit: The Chrysalis Program: www.thedarkbrowngirl.com

Affirmations have dual benefits.

- The first is that it speaks each statement into existence. Words have power. When you speak something into the atmosphere it begins to manifest.

- The second purpose is to combat negative self talk. The best way to allow our minds to change the channel from the thought that we aren't good enough (for whatever reason), is to allow ourselves to hear positive self-affirmations.

The Chrysalis Program teaches life skills, leadership, and self confidence to African American girls age 5-17 through interactive workshops. It has been a safe space for not only our students, but their parents and our volunteers.

This led to a development of a community of support that allows black women to come together to heal, grow, and be empowered. To join the movement, and visit my website: www.ashavntim.com

The Dark Brown Girl
5 Year Anniversary
Gold Edition

This 5 Year Anniversary Edition commemorates the achievements The Dark Brown Girl movement has made since it was written. We have sparked a conversation that has changed the world one readers at time.

The **DARK** Brown Girl collection celebrates children of color and their unique features and attributes. Encouraging self love and cultural pride, the collection explores subject matter

that is rarely covered in children's books.

As a mom of three beautiful brown girls, I found it difficult to find books where my children were represented. I write for them. These books say to the readers exactly what I say to my own children. Always positive, always encouraging and always written with love, these books will touch the hearts and self esteem of brown girls around the world.

Made in the USA
Monee, IL
01 March 2021